Open Weave fashions™

TAMMY HILDEBRAND

Contents

Burnt Orange Cropped Jacket

SKILL LEVEL
■■■□
INTERMEDIATE

FINISHED SIZES
Instructions given fit size small; changes for medium, large, X-large and 2X-large are in [ ].

FINISHED MEASUREMENTS
Bust: 36 inches *(small)* [40 inches *(medium)*, 44 inches *(large)*, 48 inches *(X-large)*, 52 inches *(2X-large)*]

Length: 11½ inches *(small)*, [13 inches *(medium)*, 13 inches *(large)*, 13 inches *(X-large)*, 14½ inches *(2X-large)*]

MATERIALS
- Be Sweet Bamboo light (DK) weight bamboo yarn (1¾ oz/110 yds/50g per ball): 6 [7, 7, 8, 8] balls #662 tiger
- Size G/6/4mm crochet hook or size needed to obtain gauge
- Tapestry needle
- Sewing needle
- ⅞-inch decorative shank button
- Matching sewing thread

GAUGE
Small: Ch-5 motif = 3½ inches

Medium, Large and X-Large: Ch-7 motif = 4 inches

2X-Large: Ch-11 motif = 4½ inches

16 sc rows and 8 dc rows = 4 inches

PATTERN NOTES
Weave in loose ends as work progresses.

Join with slip stitch as indicated unless otherwise stated.

Chain-3 at beginning of row counts as first double crochet unless otherwise stated.

Motifs are assembled into 2 strips of 7 motifs each and 5 strips of 3 motifs each. Strips are then sewn together with sleeves worked directly into armhole openings.

SPECIAL STITCHES
Chain-5 join (ch-5 join): Ch 2, drop lp from hook, insert hook in 2nd ch of corresponding ch-3 on previous motif, pick up dropped lp and pull through, ch 2.

Chain-3 join (ch-3 join): Ch 1, drop lp from hook, insert hook in 2nd ch of corresponding ch-3 on previous motif, pick up dropped lp and pull through, ch 1.

Cross stitch (cross st): Sk next st, dc in next st, working over dc just made, dc in sk st.

JACKET
LONG STRIP
Make 2.

FIRST MOTIF
Rnd 1 (RS): Ch 8, **join** *(see Pattern Notes)* in first ch to form ring, ch 1, 2 sc in each ch around, join in beg sc. *(16 sc)*

Rnd 2: Ch 5 [7, 7, 7, 11], sl st in same st as joining, sk next st, *(sl st, ch 5 [7, 7, 7, 11], sl st) in next st, sk next st, rep from * around, join in beg sc. *(8 ch sps)*

Rnd 3: Sl st in next st, sl st in each of first 3 [4, 4, 4, 6] chs of next ch sp, ch 1, sc in same ch sp, ch 5, *sc in next ch sp, ch 5, rep from * around, join in beg sc. *(8 sc, 8 ch-5 sps)*

Rnd 4: Sl st in next ch-5 sp, ch 1, (3 sc, ch 3, sc, ch 5, sc, ch 3, 3 sc) in same sp as beg ch-1 *(corner made)*, (3 sc, ch 3, 3 sc) in next ch-5 sp, *(3 sc, ch 3, sc, ch 5, sc, ch 3, 3 sc) in next ch-5 sp *(corner made)*, (3 sc, ch 3, 3 sc) in next ch-5 sp, rep from * around, join in beg sc. Fasten off. *(56 sc, 12 ch-3 sps, 4 ch-5 sps)*

2ND MOTIF

Rnds 1–3: Rep rnds 1–3 of First Motif.

Rnd 4: Sl st in next ch-5 sp, ch 1, (3 sc, ch 3, sc, **ch-5 join**—see *Special Stitches*, in any ch-5 sp of any corner on previous motif, sc, **ch-3 join**— *see Special Stitches*, in next ch-3 sp on previous motif, 3 sc) in same sp as beg ch-1, (3 sc, ch-3 join in next ch-3 sp on previous motif, 3 sc) in next ch-3 sp, (3 sc, ch 1, sl st in next ch-3 sp on previous motif, ch 1, sc, ch 2, sl st in next ch-5 sp on previous motif, ch 2, sc, ch 3, 3 sc) in ch-5 sp of next corner *(corner made)*, (3 sc, ch 3, 3 sc) in next ch-5 sp, *(3 sc, ch 3, sc, ch 5, sc, ch 3, 3 sc) in next ch-5 sp, (3 sc, ch 3, 3 sc) in next ch-5 sp, rep from * around, join with sl st in beg sc. Fasten off. *(56 sc, 12 ch-3 sps, 4 ch-5 sps)*

3RD MOTIF

Rnds 1–3: Rep rnds 1–3 of First Motif.

Rnd 4: Sl st in next ch-5 sp, ch 1, (3 sc, ch 3, sc, ch 2, sl st in any ch-5 sp of any corner on previous motif, ch 2, sc, ch 1, sl st in next ch-3 sp on previous motif, ch 1, 3 sc) in same sp as beg ch-1, (3 sc, ch 1, sl st in next ch-3 sp on previous motif, ch 1, 3 sc) in next ch-3 sp, (3 sc, ch 1, sl st in next ch-3 sp on previous motif, ch 1, sc, ch 2, sl st in next ch-5

sp on previous motif, ch 2, sc, ch 3, 3 sc) in ch-5 sp of next corner (*corner made*), (3 sc, ch 3, 3 sc) in next ch-5 sp, *(3 sc, ch 3, sc, ch 5, sc, ch 3, 3 sc) in next ch-5 sp, (3 sc, ch 3, 3 sc) in next ch-5 sp, rep from * around, join in beg-sc. Fasten off. (*56 sc, 12 ch-3 sps, 4 ch-5 sps*)

4TH–7TH MOTIFS
Work same as 3rd Motif.

STRIP EDGING
Row 1: With RS facing, join yarn in corner ch-5 sp at either end of Strip, **ch 3** (*see Pattern Notes*), dc in same sp as beg ch-3, [2 dc in next ch-3 sp, sk next 2 sts, **cross st** (*see Special Stitches*)] twice, 2 dc in next ch-3 sp, *2 dc in center of motif joining, [2 dc in next ch-3 sp, sk next 2 sts, cross st] twice, 2 dc in next ch-3 sp, rep from * across to last ch-5 sp, 2 dc in last ch-5 sp, turn.

SIZES SMALL & MEDIUM ONLY
Fasten off.

SIZE LARGE ONLY
Row [2]: Ch 1, sc in each st across. Fasten off.

SIZES X-LARGE & 2X-LARGE ONLY
Row [2]: Ch 1, sc in each st across, turn.

Row [3]: Rep row 2. Fasten off.

SHORT STRIP
Make 4.

Work same as Long Strip through 3rd Motif.

ASSEMBLY
With RS facing and referring to Assembly Diagram for placement, sew Motifs tog. With RS facing and matching sts of edging, fold piece in half at shoulder and sew bottom 18 sts tog for side seam. Rep for 2nd side.

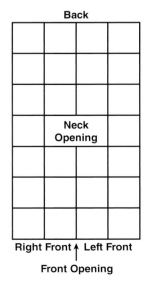

Burnt Ombre Cropped Jacket
Assembly Diagram

NECK SHAPING
SIZES SMALL, MEDIUM & LARGE ONLY
Row 1: With RS facing, join yarn with sc in sp formed by last st of strip edging on top of right front, sc in next 0 (0, 1) row(s), sc in next ch-5 sp, [sc in next ch-3 sp, sk next 2 sts, cross st] twice, sc in next ch-3 sp, sc in next ch-5 sp, sc in center of strip joining, [cross st] 5 times, sc in center of strip joining, sc in next ch-5 sp, sc in next ch-3 sp, [sk next 2 sts, cross st, sc in next ch-3 sp] twice, sc in next ch-5 sp, sc in center of strip joining, sc in next ch-5 sp, [sk next 2 sts, cross st, sc in next ch-3 sp] twice, sc in next ch-5 sp, sc in center of strip joining, [cross st] 5 times, sc in center of strip joining, sc in next ch-5 sp, sc in next ch-3 sp, [sk next 2 sts, cross st, sc in next ch-3 sp] twice, sc in next ch-5 sp, sc in sp formed by last st of each row of strip edging on top of left front, turn.

SIZES X-LARGE & 2X-LARGE ONLY
Row [1]: With RS facing, join yarn with sc in sp formed by last st of strip edging on top of right front, sc in each of next 2 rows, sc in next ch-5 sp, [sc in next ch-3 sp, sk next 2 sts, cross st] twice, sc in next ch-3 sp, sc in next ch-5 sp, sk next row, sc in next row, sc in center of strip joining, sk next row, sc in next row, [cross st] 5 times, sk next row, sc in next row, sc in center of strip joining, sk next row, sc in next row, sc in next ch-5 sp, sc in next ch-3 sp, [sk next 2 sts, cross st, sc in next ch-3 sp] twice, sc in next ch-5 sp, sk next row, sc in next row, sc in center of strip joining, sk next row, sc in next row, sc in next ch-5 sp, [sk next 2 sts, cross st, sc in next ch-3 sp] twice, sc in next ch-5 sp, sk next row, sc in next row, sc in center of strip joining, sk next row, sc in next row, [cross st] 5 times, sk next row, sc in next row, sc in center of strip joining, sk next row, sc in next row, sc in next ch-5 sp, sc in next ch-3 sp, [sk next 2 sts, cross st, sc in next ch-3 sp] twice, sc in next ch-5 sp, sc in sp formed by last st of each row of strip edging on top of left front, turn.

ALL SIZES
Row 2: Ch 1, sc in each st across. Fasten off.

SLEEVE
Rnd 1: With RS facing, join yarn with sc in center of side seam, [**sc dec** (*see Stitch Guide*) in next 2 sts] 1 [1, 1, 2, 2] time(s), [cross st]

23 times, [sc dec in next 2 sts] 1 [1, 1, 2, 2] time(s), join in beg sc. (3 [3, 3, 5, 5] sc, 23 cross sts)

Rnd 2: Sl st in each of next 3 sts, ch 3, dc in previous st, cross st to last 2 sts, sc dec in last 2 sts, join in 3rd ch of beg ch-3. (1 sc, 23 [23, 23, 25, 25] cross sts)

Rnds 3–37: Sl st in next st, ch 3, dc in previous st, cross st around, join in 3rd ch of beg ch-3. At end of last rnd, fasten off. (23 [23, 23, 25, 25] cross sts)

Rep for 2nd sleeve.

BOTTOM BORDER
SIZES SMALL, MEDIUM & LARGE ONLY
Row 1: With RS facing, join yarn in sp formed by st of last row of strip edging at bottom of left front, ch 3, dc in same sp, 2 dc in next ch-5 sp, [2 dc in next ch-3 sp, sk next 2 sts, cross st] twice, 2 dc in next ch-3 sp, 2 dc in next ch-5 sp, *2 dc in center of strip joining, 2 dc in next ch-5 sp, [2 dc in next ch-3 sp, sk next 2 sts, cross st] twice, 2 dc in next ch-3 sp, 2 dc in next ch-5 sp, rep from * across, 2 dc in last row of strip edging, turn.

SIZES X-LARGE & 2X-LARGE ONLY
Row [1]: With RS facing, join yarn in sp formed by st of last row of strip edging at bottom of left front, sk next row, 2 dc in next row, ch 3, dc in same sp, 2 dc in next ch-5 sp, [2 dc in next ch-3 sp, skip next 2 sts, cross st] twice, 2 dc in next ch-3 sp, 2 dc in next ch-5 sp, *sk next row, 2 dc in next row, 2 dc in center of strip joining, sk next row, 2 dc in next row, 2 dc in next ch-5 sp, [2 dc in next ch-3 sp, sk next 2 sts, cross st] twice, 2 dc in next ch-3 sp, 2 dc in next ch-5 sp, rep from * across, sk next row, 2 dc in each of next 2 rows of strip edging, turn.

ALL SIZES
Row 2: Ch 1, sc in each st across. Fasten off.

FINISHING
Immerse in cool water, squeeze out excess water, taking care not to wring or twist. Place the piece on a flat, covered surface, gently stretching to open lace pattern. Leave until completely dry. Sew button to top left at neck. ∎

Once Upon A Dream Shawl

SKILL LEVEL

INTERMEDIATE

FINISHED MEASUREMENTS

23¾ inches wide x 61 inches long

MATERIALS

- Wisdom Yarns Poems Silk medium (worsted) weight wool/silk yarn (1¾ oz/109 yds/50g per skein): 7 skeins #805 all the way
- Size I/9/5.5mm crochet hook
- Tapestry needle

GAUGE

Gauge is not important for this project.

PATTERN NOTES

Weave in loose ends as work progresses.

Join with slip stitch as indicated unless otherwise stated.

Chain-3 at beginning of round or row counts as first double crochet unless otherwise stated.

Chain-4 at beginning of round or row counts as first double crochet and chain-1 unless otherwise stated.

Completed strips will have a slight lean which can be straightened when piece is blocked.

SPECIAL STITCH

Chain-3 join (ch-3 join): Ch 1, drop lp from hook, insert hook in 2nd ch of corresponding ch-3 sp on previous strip, pick up dropped lp and pull through, ch 1.

SHAWL

STRIP
Make 5.

BASIC CIRCLE

Rnd 1: Ch 6, **join** (see Pattern Notes) in first ch to form ring, **ch 3** (see Pattern Notes), 15 dc in ring, join in 3rd ch of beg ch-3, turn. (16 dc)

Rnd 2: Ch 4 (see Pattern Notes), *dc in next st, ch 1, rep from * around, join in 3rd ch of beg ch-4, turn. (16 dc, 16 ch-1 sps)

Rnd 3: Ch 1, (sc, ch 3, sc) in each ch-1 sp around, join in beg sc. (32 sc, 16 ch-3 sps)

FIRST HALF CIRCLE

Row 1: Ch 6, turn, sl st in same st as joining, turn, sl st in ch-6 sp, ch 3, 7 dc in ring, turn. (8 dc)

Row 2: Ch 4, dc in next st, *ch 1, dc in next st, rep from * across, turn. (8 dc, 7 ch-1 sps)

Row 3: Ch 1, sc in next ch-1 sp, ch 1, turn, sk first unworked ch-3 sp on Base Circle from joining, sl st in 2nd ch of next ch-3 sp on Base Circle, ch 1, turn, sc in same ch-1 sp on working circle, (sc, ch 3, sc) in each rem ch-1 sp on working circle. Do not turn.

2ND HALF CIRCLE

Row 1: Ch 6, sl st in top of last st on row 1 of previous half circle to form ring, turn, sl st in ring, ch 3, 7 dc in ring, turn. (8 dc)

Row 2: Ch 4, dc in next st, *ch 1, dc in next st, rep from * across, turn. (8 dc, 7 ch-1 sps)

Row 3: Ch 1, sc in next ch-1 sp, ch 1, turn, to join to Base Circle, sk first unworked ch-3 sp on Base Circle, sl st in 2nd ch of next ch-3 sp, ch 1, turn, sc in same ch-1 sp on working circle, (sc, ch 3, sc) in each rem ch-1 sp across. Do not turn.

3RD HALF CIRCLE

Row 1: Ch 6, sl st in top of last st on row 1 of previous half circle to form ring, turn, sl st in ring, ch 3, 7 dc in ring, turn. *(8 dc)*

Row 2: Ch 4, dc in next st, *ch 1, dc in next st, rep from * across, turn. *(8 dc, 7 ch-1 sps)*

Row 3: Ch 1, turn, sc in next ch-1 sp, ch 1, turn, to join to previous half circle, sk first unworked ch-3 sp on previous half circle, sl st in 2nd ch of next ch-3 sp, ch 1, turn, sc in same ch-1 sp on working half circle, (sc, ch 3, sc) in each rem ch-3 sp on working half circle. Do not turn.

4TH–23RD HALF CIRCLES

Work same as 3rd Half Circle.

LAST CIRCLE

Row 1: Ch 6, sl st in top of last st on row 1 of previous half circle to form ring, turn, sl st in ring, ch 3, 14 dc in ring. *(15 dc)*

Row 2: Ch 4, *dc in next st, ch 1, rep from * around, join in 3rd ch of beg ch-4, turn. *(15 dc, 14 ch-1 sps)*

Row 3: Ch 1, sc in next ch-1 sp, ch 1, turn, to join to previous half circle, sk first unworked ch-3 sp on previous half circle, sl st in 2nd ch of next ch-3 sp, ch 1, turn, sc in same ch-1 sp on working half circle, (sc, ch 3, sc) in each of next 12 ch-1 sps, sc in next ch-1 sp, ch 1, to join to previous half circle on opposite side, sk next ch-3 sp, sl st in 2nd ch of next ch-3 sp, ch 1, sc in last ch-1 sp on working circle.

FIRST STRIP EDGING

Rnd 1: Sl st in same sp as joining, ch 4 *(counts as tr)*, *[(dc, ch 3, dc) in next ch-3 sp, (sc, ch 3, sc) in each of next 2 ch-3 sps, (dc, ch 3, dc) in next ch-3 sp, tr in center of next joining] 14 times, (dc, ch 3, dc) in next ch-3 sp, (sc, ch 3, sc) in each of next 2 ch-3 sps, [dc, (ch 3, dc) 3 times] in next ch-3 sp, (sc, ch 3, sc) in each of next 4 ch-3 sps, [dc, (ch 3, dc) 3 times] in next ch-3 sp, (sc, ch 3, sc) in each of next 2 ch-3 sps, (dc, ch 3, dc) in next ch-3 sp**, tr in center of next joining, rep from * once, ending rep at **, join in 4th ch of beg ch-4. Fasten off.

STRIPS 2–5 EDGING

Rnd 1: Sl st in same sp as joining, ch 4, *(dc, ch 3, dc) in next ch-3 sp, (sc, ch 3, sc) in next 2 ch-3 sps, (dc, ch 3, dc) in next ch-3 sp, tr in center of next joining, rep from * 13 times, (dc, ch 3, dc) in next ch-3 sp, (sc, ch 3, sc) in each of next 2 ch-3 sps, [dc, (ch 3, dc) 3 times] in next ch-3 sp, (sc, ch 3, sc) in each of next 4 ch-3 sps, [dc, ch 3, dc, (**ch-3 join**—*see Special Stitch*, dc) twice] in next ch-3 sp, (sc, ch-3 join, sc) in each of next 2 ch-3 sps, (dc, ch-3 join, dc) in next ch-3 sp, tr in center of next joining, **(dc, ch-3 join, dc) in next ch-3 sp, (sc, ch-3 join, sc) in each of next 2 ch-3 sps, (dc, ch-3 join, dc) in next ch-3 sp, tr in center of next joining; rep from ** 13 times, (dc, ch-3 join, dc) in next ch-3 sp, (sc, ch-3 join, sc) in each of next 2 ch-3 sps, [dc, (ch-3 join, dc) twice, ch 3, dc] in next ch-3 sp, (sc, ch 3, sc) in each of next 4 ch-3 sps, [dc, (ch 3, dc) 3 times] in next ch-3 sp, (sc, ch 3, sc) in each of next 2 ch-3 sps, (dc, ch 3, dc) in next ch-3 sp, join in 4th ch of beg ch-4. Fasten off.

FINISHING

Immerse in cool water, squeeze out excess water, taking care not to wring or twist. Place the piece on a flat, covered surface, gently stretching to open lace pattern and square up strips. Leave until completely dry. ■

Red Hot Tunic

SKILL LEVEL

INTERMEDIATE

FINISHED SIZES

Instructions given fit size small; changes for medium, large, X-large, 2X-large and 3X-large are in [ ].

FINISHED MEASUREMENTS

Bust: 31½ inches *(small)* [36 inches *(medium)*, 40½ inches *(large)*, 45 inches *(X-large)*, 50 inches *(2X-large)*, 55 inches *(3X-large)*]

Length: 26 inches

MATERIALS

- Tahki Yarns Cotton Classic Lite fine (sport) weight cotton yarn (1¾ oz/ 146 yds/50g per hank):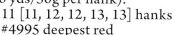
    11 [11, 12, 12, 13, 13] hanks
    #4995 deepest red
- Size F/5/3.75mm crochet hook or size needed to obtain gauge
- Tapestry needle

GAUGE

16 sc = 4 inches; 18 sc rows = 4 inches

PATTERN NOTES

Weave in loose ends as work progresses.

Join with slip stitch as indicated unless otherwise stated.

Chain-4 at beginning of round counts as first double crochet and chain-1 unless otherwise stated.

Chain-3 at beginning of round counts as first double crochet unless otherwise stated.

Individual strips are made then assembled using a join-as-you-go technique. Sleeves are worked directly in armhole openings.

SPECIAL STITCH

Chain-3 join (ch-3 join): Ch 1, drop lp from hook, insert hook in 2nd ch of corresponding ch-3 sp on previous strip, pick up dropped lp and pull through, ch 1.

TUNIC
STRIP A
Make 8.

Row 1: Starting at top, ch 4 [5, 6, 7, 7, 8], sc in 2nd ch from hook and in each ch across, turn. *(3 [4, 5, 6, 6, 7] sc)*

Rows 2–61: Ch 1, sc in each st across, turn.

Row 62: Ch 1, 2 sc in first st, sc in each st to last st, 2 sc in last st, turn. *(5 [6, 7, 8, 8, 9] sc)*

Rows 63–81: Rep row 2.

Rows 82–101: Rep rows 62–81. *(7 [8, 9, 10, 10, 11] sc at end of last row)*

Rows 102–121: Rep rows 62–81. *(9 [10, 11, 12, 12, 13] sc at end of last row)*

FIRST SIDE EDGING
Row 1: Ch 1, working across next side in ends of rows, sc in each row across, turn. *(121 sc)*

Row 2: Ch 1, sc in first st, *ch 3, sk next st, sc in next st, rep from * across. Do not turn. *(61 sc, 60 ch-3 sps)*

STRIP B
Make 10.

Row 1: Ch 4 [5, 6, 7, 7, 8], sc in 2nd ch from hook and in each ch across, turn. *(3 [4, 5, 6, 6, 7] sc)*

Rows 2–41: Ch 1, sc in each st across, turn.

Row 42: Ch 1, 2 sc in first st, sc in each st to last st, 2 sc in last st, turn. *(5 [6, 7, 8, 8, 9] sc)*

Rows 43–61: Rep row 2.

Rows 62–81: Rep rows 42–61. *(7 [8, 9, 10, 10, 11] sc)*

Rows 82–101: Rep rows 42–61. *(9 [10, 11, 12, 12, 13] sc at end of last row)*

FIRST SIDE EDGING
Row 1: Ch 1, working across next side in ends of rows, sc in each row across, turn. *(101 sc)*

Row 2: Ch 1, sc in first st, *ch 3, sk next st, sc in next st, rep from * across. Fasten off. *(51 sc, 50 ch-3 sps)*

STRIP C
SIZES 2X-LARGE & 3X-LARGE ONLY
Make 2.

Row [1]: Ch 7 [8], sc in 2nd ch from hook and in each ch across, turn. *(6 [7] sc)*

Rows [2–33]: Ch 1, sc in each st across, turn.

Row [34]: Ch 1, 2 sc in first st, sc in each st to last st, 2 sc in last st, turn. *(8 [9] sc)*

Rows [35–53]: Rep row 2.

Rows [54–73]: Rep rows 34–53. *(10 [11] sc at end of last row)*

Rows [74–93]: Rep rows 54–73. *(11 [12] sc at end of last row)*

FIRST SIDE EDGING
Row 1: Ch 1, working across next side in ends of rows, sc in each row across, turn. *(93 sc)*

Row 2: Ch 1, sc in first st, *ch 3, sk next st, sc in next st, rep from * across. Fasten off. *(47 sc, 46 ch-3 sps)*

ASSEMBLY
Note: Refer to Assembly Diagrams for placement of strips.

FIRST LONG STRIP
2ND SIDE EDGING
Row 1: With RS facing, working in ends of rows across unedged side, join yarn with sc in row 121, sc in each row across, turn.

Row 2: Ch 1, sc in first st, *ch 3, sk next st, sc in next st, rep from * across. Fasten off.

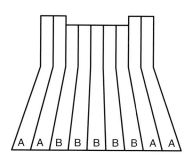

Red Hot Tunic
Assembly Diagram A

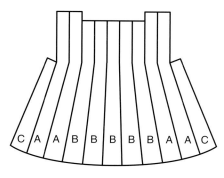

Red Hot Tunic
Assembly Diagram B

2ND LONG STRIP
2ND SIDE EDGING
Row 1: With RS facing, working in ends of rows across unedged side, join yarn with sc in row 121, sc in each row across, turn.

Row 2: Ch 1, sc in first st, *ch-3 join (see Special Stitch), sk next st, sc in next st, rep from * across. Fasten off.

FIRST SHORT STRIP
2ND SIDE EDGING
Row 1: With RS facing, working in ends of rows across unedged side, join yarn with sc in row 121, sc in each row across, turn.

Row 2: Ch 1, sc in first st, sk first 9 ch-3 sps on previous strip, ch-3 join in next ch-3 sp on previous strip, sk next st on working strip, sc in next st, *ch-3 join, sk next st, sc in next st, rep from * across. Fasten off.

REM SHORT STRIPS
Work edging same as 2nd Side Edging of 2nd Long Strip.

3RD LONG STRIP
2ND SIDE EDGING
Row 1: With RS facing, working in ends of rows across unedged side, join yarn with sc in row 121, sc in each row across, turn.

Row 2: Ch 1, sc in first st, [ch 3, sk next st, sc in next st] 9 times, ch-3 join in first ch-3 sp on previous short strip, sk next st on working strip, sc in next st, *ch-3 join, sk next st, sc in next st, rep from * across. Fasten off.

4TH LONG STRIP
2ND SIDE EDGING
Work same as 2nd Side Edging of First Long Strip.

SHOULDER
With RS facing and short end of long strips at top, join yarn with sc in first row of edging on right-hand side, sc in next row, working in unused lps on opposite side of foundation ch, sc in each of next 3 [4, 5, 6, 6, 7] chs, sc in each of next 2 rows of edging, sc in each of next 2 row ends on next long strip, working in unused lps on opposite side of foundation ch, sc in each of next 3 [4, 5, 6, 6, 7] chs, sc in each of next 2 rows of edging. Fasten off.

Rep with rem long strips.

ASSEMBLY
With yarn needle, matching up front and back, sew shoulder seams.

SIDE SEAM
Row 1: Join (see Pattern Notes) yarn in ch-3 sp at bottom on right-hand side of either front or back, ch 4, drop lp from hook, insert hook in center ch of corresponding ch-3 on opposite panel, pick up dropped lp and pull through, ch 1, dc in same ch-3 sp on first panel, *(dc, ch-3 join, dc) in next ch-3 sp on first panel, rep from * 45 times. Fasten off.

Rep for 2nd side seam.

NECK SHAPING

Rnd 1: With RS facing, join yarn with sc in first ch-3 sp on either shoulder, *[ch 1, sc in next ch-3 sp] 19 times, working in unused lps of foundation chs of Strip B, sc in each of next 3 [4, 5, 6, 6, 7] sts, [(dc, ch 1, dc) in center of strip joining, sc in each of next 3 [4, 5, 6, 6, 7] sts] 4 times, rep from * once, join in beg sc.

Rnd 2: Ch 1, sc in first st, *[ch 1, sc in next sc] 19 times, sc in next 1 [0, 1, 0, 0, 1] st(s), [**sc dec** *(see Stitch Guide)* in next 2 sts] 1 [2, 2, 3, 3, 3] time(s), [(dc, ch 1, dc) in next ch-1 sp, sc in next 1 [0, 1, 0, 0, 1] st(s), [(sc dec in next 2 sts) 1 [2, 2, 3, 3, 3] time(s)] 4 times, sc in next st, rep from * once, join in beg sc.

Rnd 3: Ch 1, sc in first st, *[ch 1, sc in next sc] 19 times, sc in each of next 2 [2, 3, 3, 3, 4] sts, [(dc, ch 1, dc) in next ch-1 sp, sc in each of next 2 [2, 3, 3, 3, 4] sts] 4 times, sc in next st, rep from * once join in beg sc. Fasten off.

BOTTOM BORDER

Rnd 1: With RS facing, join yarn in row end of either side seam at bottom edge, **ch 4** *(see Pattern Notes)*, [dc, (ch 1, dc) twice] in same sp as beg ch-4, sc in each st across last row of next strip, *[dc, (ch 1, dc) 3 times] in center of strip joining, sc in each st across last row of next strip, rep from * around, join in 3rd ch of beg ch-4.

Rnd 2: Ch 1, sc in each st and ch around, join in beg sc. Fasten off.

SLEEVE
SIZES SMALL, MEDIUM, LARGE & X-LARGE ONLY

Rnd 1: With RS facing, join yarn with sc in row end of side seam at underarm, working around armhole opening, sc in each of next 2 ch-3 sps, 2 dc in each of next 24 ch-3 sps, sc in each of next 2 ch-3 sps, join in beg sc. *(5 sc, 48 dc)*

Rnd 2: Ch 1, sc in first st, sc dec in next 2 sts, [sc in next st, ch 2, sk next st] 24 times, sk next st, sc dec in next 2 sts, join in beg sc. *(27 sc, 24 ch-2 sps)*

Rnd 3: Ch 1, sc in first st, 2 dc in each ch-2 sp around, join in beg sc. *(1 sc, 48 dc)*

Rnd 4: Ch 1, sc in same st as beg ch-1, ch 2, sk next st, *sc in next st, ch 2, sk next st, rep from * around, join in beg sc. *(24 sc, 24 ch-2 sps)*

Rnd 5: Sl st in next ch-2 sp, **ch 3** *(see Pattern Notes)*, dc in same sp, 2 dc in each rem ch-2 sp around, join in beg sc.

Rnds 6–15: [Rep rnds 4 and 5 alternately] 5 times. At end of last rnd, fasten off.

Rep around 2nd armhole.

SIZES 2X-LARGE & 3X-LARGE ONLY

Rnd [1]: With RS facing, working in bottom lps of row 1 on underarm strip, join yarn with sc in first st, [sc dec in next 2 sts] 2 [3] times, sc in next 0 [1] st(s), sc in end of row of side seam, working around armhole opening, sc in each of next 2 ch-3 sps, 2 dc in each of next 24 ch-3 sps, sc in each of next 2 ch-3 sps, join in beg sc. *(9 sc, 48 dc)*

Rnd [2]: Ch 1, [sc dec in next 2 sts] twice, [sc in next st, ch 2, sk next st] 24 times, sk next st, sc dec in next 2 sts, join in beg sc. *(27 sc, 24 ch-2 sps)*

Rnd [3]: Ch 1, sc in first st, 2 dc in each ch-2 sp around, join in beg sc. *(1 sc, 48 dc)*

Rnd [4]: Ch 1, sc in same st, ch 2, sk next st, *sc in next st, ch 2, sk next st, rep from * around, join in beg sc. *(24 sc, 24 ch-2 sps)*

Rnd [5]: Sl st in next ch-2 sp, ch 3, dc in same sp as beg ch-3, 2 dc in each rem ch-2 sp around, join in 3rd ch of beg ch-3. *(48 dc)*

Rnds [6–15]: [Rep rnds 4 and 5 alternately] 5 times. At end of last rnd, fasten off.

Rep around 2nd armhole.

FINISHING

Immerse in cool water, squeeze out excess water, taking care not to wring or twist. Place the piece on a flat, covered surface. Leave until completely dry. ∎

Verde Recherché Duster

SKILL LEVEL

INTERMEDIATE

FINISHED SIZES

Instructions given fit size small; changes for medium, large, X-large, 2X-large and 3X-large are in [ ].

FINISHED MEASUREMENTS

Bust: 37 inches *(small)* [41 inches *(medium)*, 45 inches *(large)*, 49 inches *(X-large)*, 53 inches *(2X-large)*, 57 inches *(3X-large)*]

Length: 28½ inches

MATERIALS

- Omega Sinfonia fine (sport) weight cotton yarn (3½ oz/218 yds/100g per skein):
  6 [6, 7, 7, 8, 8] skeins #880 green
- Size I/9/5.5mm crochet hook or size needed to obtain gauge
- Tapestry needle

GAUGE

2 shells = 3½ inches; 16 rows = 4 inches

In lace pattern: 5 rows = 4 inches

PATTERN NOTES

Duster is made in 2 identical panels worked from end of sleeve to center of back then both panels are joined together at center of back using a join-as-you-go technique. Sleeve and side seams are then assembled using a join-as-you-go technique.

Weave in loose ends as work progresses.

Chain-4 at beginning of row counts as first double crochet and chain-1 unless otherwise stated.

Join with slip stitch as indicated unless otherwise stated.

Chain-6 at beginning of row counts as
first double crochet and chain-3 unless otherwise stated.

SPECIAL STITCHES

Cluster (cl): Holding back last lp of each dc on
hook, 2 dc in indicated st, yo and draw through
all 3 lps on hook.

Shell: (**Cl** (*see Special Stitches*), ch 1, dc, ch 1, cl)
in same st.

Chain-3 join (ch-3 join): Ch 1, drop lp from hook,
insert hook in 2nd ch of corresponding ch-3 sp,
pick up dropped lp and pull through, ch 1.

DUSTER
FIRST PANEL
SLEEVE
Row 1 (RS): Beg at end of sleeve, ch 45 [45, 50,
50, 55, 55], **cl** (*see Special Stitches*) in 5th ch
from hook, sk next 4 chs, *shell (*see Special
Stitches*) in next ch, sk next 4 chs, rep from *
7 [7, 8, 8, 9, 9] times, (cl, ch 1, dc) in last ch,
turn. (*7 [7, 8, 8, 9, 9] shells, 2 dc, 2 cls*)

Row 2: Ch 4 (*see Pattern Notes*), dc in next ch-1
sp, *ch 3, sc in sp before next shell, ch 3, dc in
next ch-1 sp, ch 1, dc in next ch-1 sp, rep from
* 6 [6, 7, 7, 8, 8] times, ch 3, sc in sp before next
cl, ch 3, dc in next ch-1 sp, ch 1, dc in 3rd ch of
beg ch-4, turn.

Row 3: Ch 4, cl in first ch-1 sp, *shell in next
ch-1 sp; rep from * 7 [7, 8, 8, 9, 9] times, cl in
next ch-1 sp, ch 1, dc in 3rd ch of beg ch-4, turn.

Rows 4–23: [Rep rows 2 and 3 alternately]
10 times.

FRONT & BACK
Row 1: Ch 4, dc in first ch-1 sp, *ch 3, sc in sp
before next shell, ch 3, dc in next ch-1 sp, ch 1,
dc in next ch-1 sp, rep from * 6 times, ch 3, sc in
sp before next cl, ch 3, dc in next ch-1 sp, ch 1,
dc in 3rd ch of turning ch, drop lp from hook,
with separate skein of yarn, **join** (*see Pattern
Notes*) in 3rd ch of beg ch-4 of row, ch 75, fasten
off, pick up dropped lp, ch 79, turn.

Row 2: Cl in 5th ch from hook, sk next 4 chs, [shell in next ch, sk next 4 chs] 14 times, shell in each of next 9 [9, 10, 10, 11, 11] ch-1 sps, sk next 4 chs, [shell in next ch, sk next 4 chs] 14 times, (shell, ch 1, dc) in last ch, turn. (37 [37, 38, 38, 39, 39] shells, 2 cls, 2 dc)

Row 3: Ch 4, dc in first ch-1 sp, *ch 3, sc in sp before next shell, ch 3, dc in next ch-1 sp, ch 1, dc in next ch-1 sp, rep from *36 [36, 37, 37, 38, 38] times, ch 3, sc in sp before next cl, ch 3, dc in next ch-1 sp, ch 1, dc in 3rd ch of beg ch-4, turn.

Row 4: Ch 4, cl in next ch-1 sp, *shell in next ch-1 sp, rep from * 37 [37, 38, 38, 39, 39] times, cl in next ch-1 sp, ch 1, dc in 3rd ch of beg ch-4, turn.

Rows 5–10 [5–12, 5–12, 5–14, 5–14, 5–16]: [Rep rows 3 and 4 alternately] 3 [4, 4, 5, 5, 6] times.

SIZES SMALL, LARGE & 2X-LARGE ONLY
Row 11 [13, 15]: Rep row 3.

Row 12 [14, 16]: Ch 1, (sc, ch 3, sc) in first ch-1 sp, *ch 1, dc in next sc, ch 1, (sc, ch 3, sc) in next ch-1 sp, rep from * across, turn.

SIZES MEDIUM, X-LARGE & 3X-LARGE ONLY
Row [13, 15, 17]: Ch 1, (sc, ch 3, sc) in first ch-1 sp, *dc in sp before next shell, sc in next ch-1 sp, ch 3, sc in next ch-1 sp, rep from * across to last cl, dc in sp before last cl, (sc, ch 3, sc) in last ch-1 sp, turn.

ALL SIZES
Row 13 [14, 15, 16, 17, 18]: Ch 1, (sc, ch 3, sc) in first ch-3 sp, *(sc, ch 3, sc) in next dc, (sc, ch 3, sc) in next ch-3 sp, rep from * across, turn.

Row(s) 14 [15 & 16, 16–18, 17–20, 18–22, 19–24]: Ch 1, (sc, ch 3, sc) in first ch-3 sp and in each rem ch-3 sp across, turn.

At end of last row, fasten off.

2ND PANEL
Work same as First Panel. At end of last row, do not fasten off.

Note: Following row joins Panels tog at center back.

Joining row: Ch 1, (sc, **ch-3 join**—*see Special Stitches*, sc) in first ch-3 sp and in each of next 37 ch-3 sps, (sc, ch 3, sc) in each rem ch-3 sp on 2nd Panel. Fasten off.

FIRST SIDE SEAM EDGING
Row 1: With RS facing, fold Panels matching sleeve and side edges, working through both Panels at same time in bottom of chs and sps of row 1 of Panels, join yarn in first ch, **ch 6** (*see Pattern Notes*), dc in same ch, [(dc, ch 3, dc) in next sp, (dc, ch 3, dc) in next ch] 8 times, (sc, ch 3, sc) in next sp, [(sc, ch 3, sc) in next ch, (sc, ch 3, sc) in next sp] 6 times, working in row ends of sleeve, (sc, ch 3, sc) in each row to last row, sl st in last row. Fasten off.

2ND SIDE SEAM EDGING
Row 1: With RS facing, working in opposite side of row ends on rem sleeve, working through both thicknesses, join yarn in row 1, (sc, ch-3 join, sc) in each row, working in bottom of chs and sps of row 1 on opposite side of Panels, [(sc, ch 3, sc) in next sp, (sc, ch 3, sc) in next ch] 6 times, (dc, ch-3 join, dc) in each ch-3 sp across. Fasten off.

FINISHING
Immerse the piece in cool water, squeeze out excess water, taking care not to wring or twist. Place the piece on a flat, covered surface, gently stretching to open lace pattern. Leave until completely dry. ∎

Perfect Color Lace Pullover & Hat

SKILL LEVEL

INTERMEDIATE

PULLOVER

FINISHED SIZES

Instructions given fit size small; changes for medium, large, X-large, 2X-large and 3X-large are in [ ].

FINISHED MEASUREMENTS

Bust: 36 [40½, 45, 49½, 52½, 55½] inches

Length: 22 [22, 22, 25, 25] inches

HAT

FINISHED MEASUREMENT

22 inches in circumference

MATERIALS

- Plymouth Yarn Cleo light (DK) weight cotton yarn (1¾ oz/125 yds/ 50 grams per skein):
  - 3 [3, 4, 4, 5, 5] skeins #155 turquoise
  - 2 [2, 2, 3, 3, 3] skeins #137 tutu
  - 2 [2, 2, 3, 3, 3] skeins #138 pigtail
  - 2 [2, 2, 3, 3, 3] skeins #139 orchid
- Size H/8/5mm crochet hook or size needed to obtain gauge
- Tapestry needle

GAUGE

Rnds 1–3: 3¾ inches; 3 V-sts and 5 rows = 3¾ inches

PATTERN NOTES

Try making this pullover and hat in a solid color for a more classic, chic look. Where you would fasten off and join a new color in these instructions, simply chain 1 and continue working the pattern. See page 21 for what the pullover and hat look like crocheted in a cream yarn!

Weave in loose ends as work progresses.

Join with slip stitch as indicated unless otherwise stated.

Chain-3 at beginning of round counts as a double crochet unless otherwise stated.

Chain-4 at beginning of round counts as a double crochet and chain-1 unless otherwise stated.

Chain-6 at beginning of round counts as a double crochet and chain-3 unless otherwise stated.

SPECIAL STITCHES

Beginning V-stitch (beg V-st): Ch 6 (see Pattern Notes), dc in indicated sp.

V-stitch (V-st): (Dc, ch 3, dc) in indicated sp.

V-stitch join (V-st join): (Dc, ch 1, drop lp from hook, insert hook in 2nd ch of corresponding ch-3 sp, pick up dropped lp and pull through, ch 1, dc) in same sp.

Chain-3 join (ch-3 join): (Dc, drop lp from hook, insert hook in 2nd ch of corresponding ch-3 on indicated piece, pick up dropped lp and pull through, ch 1, dc) in indicated ch-3 sp.

PULLOVER
FRONT

Rnd 1 (RS): With tutu, ch 5, **join** (see Pattern Notes) in first ch to form ring, **ch 3** (see Pattern Notes), 15 dc in ring, join in 3rd ch of beg ch-3. (16 dc)

Rnd 2: Ch 4 (see Pattern Notes), *dc in next st, ch 1, rep from * around, join in 3rd ch of beg ch-4. Fasten off. (16 dc, 16 ch-1 sps)

Rnd 3: With RS facing, join pigtail with sc in first ch-1 sp, ch 3, sc in same sp, (sc, ch 3, sc) in each rem ch-1 sp around, join in beg sc. Fasten off. (32 sc, 16 ch-3 sps)

Rnd 4: With RS facing, join turquoise in ch-3 sp of beg V-st, ch-3 sp, **beg V-st** (see Special

Stitches), dc in same sp, **V-st** *(see Special Stitches)* in each rem ch-3 sp around, join in 3rd ch of beg ch-6. *(16 V-sts)*

Rnd 5: Sl st in next ch-3 sp, beg V-st in same sp, ch 1, *V-st in ch-3 sp of next V-st, ch 1, rep from * around, join in 3rd ch of beg ch-6. Fasten off. *(16 V-sts)*

Rnd 6: With RS facing, join orchid with sc in same sp as joining, 5 dc in ch-3 sp of next V-st, *sc in sp before next V-st, 5 dc in ch-3 sp of next V-st, rep from * around, join in beg sc. Fasten off. *(80 dc, 16 sc)*

Rnd 7: With RS facing, join pigtail in any sc, beg V-st in same st, ch 1, sk next 2 dc, sl st in next dc, ch 1, *V-st in next sc, ch 1, sk next 2 dc, sl st in next dc, ch 1, rep from * around, join in 3rd ch of beg ch-6. Fasten off. *(16 V-sts, 16 sl sts)*

Rnd 8: With RS facing, join turquoise with sc in ch-3 sp of beg V-st, ch 3, sc in same sp, ch 5, *(sc, ch 3, sc) in ch-3 sp of next V-st, ch 5, rep from * around, join in beg sc. *(32 sc, 16 ch-3 sps, 16 ch-5 sps)*

Rnd 9: Sl st in next ch-3 sp, beg V-st in same sp, ch 3, sc in next ch-5 sp, ch 3, *V-st in next ch-3 sp, ch 3, sc in next ch-5 sp, ch 3, rep from * around, join in 3rd ch of beg ch-6. Fasten off. *(16 V-sts, 16 sc)*

Rnd 10: With RS facing, join tutu in ch-3 sp of beg V-st, (beg V-st, ch 3, V-st) in same sp, ch 5, [(sc, ch 3, sc) in ch-3 sp of next V-st, ch 5] 3 times, *(V-st, ch 3, V-st) in ch-3 sp of next V-st, ch 5, [(sc, ch 3, sc) in ch-3 sp of next V-st, ch 5] 3 times, rep from * around, join in 3rd ch of beg ch-6. *(8 V-sts, 24 sc)*

Rnd 11: Sl st in next ch-3 sp, beg V-st in same sp, *(V-st, ch 3, V-st) in next ch-3 sp, V-st in ch-3 sp of next V-st, ch 3, sc in next ch-5 sp, ch 3, [V-st in next ch-3 sp, ch 3, sc in next ch-5 sp, ch 3] 3 times, V-st in ch-3 sp of next V-st, rep from * twice, (V-st, ch 3, V-st) in next ch-3 sp, V-st in ch-3 sp of next V-st, ch 3, sc in next ch-5 sp, ch 3, [V-st in next ch-3 sp, ch 3, sc in next ch-5 sp, ch 3] 3 times, join in 3rd ch of beg ch-6. Fasten off. *(28 V-sts, 16 sc)*

Rnd 12: With RS facing, join orchid in ch-3 sp of beg V-st, beg V-st in same sp, V-st in ch-3 sp of each of next 4 ch-3 sps, ch 7, [(sc, ch 3, sc) in next V-st, ch 7] 3 times, *V-st in ch-3 sp of each of next 5 ch-3 sps, ch 7, [(sc, ch 3, sc), in next V-st, ch 7] 3 times, rep from * around, join in 3rd ch of beg ch-6. *(20 V-sts, 24 sc)*

Rnd 13: Sl st in next ch-3 sp, beg V-st in same sp, V-st in ch-3 sp of next V-st, (V-st, ch 3, V-st) in ch-3 sp of next V-st *(corner made)*, V-st in ch-3 sp of each of next 2 V-sts, V-st in next ch-7 sp, [V-st in next ch-3 sp, V-st in next ch-7 sp] 3 times, *V-st in ch-3 sp of each of next 2 V-sts, (V-st, ch 3, V-st) in ch-3 sp of next V-st *(corner made)*, V-st in ch-3 sp of each of next 2 V-sts, V-st in next ch-7 sp, [V-st in ch-3 sp of next V-st, V-st in next ch-7 sp] 3 times, rep from * around, join in 3rd ch of beg ch-7. *(52 V-sts)*

SIZES SMALL, MEDIUM & LARGE ONLY
Fasten off.

SIZES X-LARGE, 2X-LARGE & 3X-LARGE ONLY

Rnd [14]: Sl st in next ch-3 sp, beg V-st in same sp, V-st in each ch-3 sp around, join in 3rd ch of beg ch-6.

Rnd [15]: Sl st in next ch-3 sp, beg V-st in same sp, V-st in ch-3 sp of each of next 2 V-sts, *(V-st, ch 3, V-st) in ch-3 sp of next V-st, V-st in ch-3 sp of each of next 13 V-sts, rep from * twice, (V-st, ch 3, V-st) in ch-3 sp of next V-st, V-st in ch-3 sp of each of next 10 V-sts. *(60 V-sts)*

Rnd [16]: Rep rnd 14.

Rnd [17]: Sl st in next ch-3 sp, beg V-st in same sp, V-st in ch-3 sp of each of next 3 V-sts, *(V-st, ch 3, V-st) in ch-3 sp of next V-st, V-st in ch-3 sp of each of next 15 V-sts, rep from * twice, (V-st, ch 3, V-st) in ch-3 sp of next V-st, V-st in ch-3 sp of each of next 11 V-sts. Fasten off. *(68 V-sts)*

RIGHT SHOULDER
Row 1: With RS facing, join pigtail in any center ch-3 corner sp, beg V-st in same sp, V-st in each of next 3 [3, 3, 5, 5, 5] ch-3 sps, leaving rem ch-3 sps unworked, turn. *(4 [4, 4, 6, 6, 6] V-sts)*

Rows 2–5: Ch 1, sl st in next ch-3 sp, beg V-st in same sp, V-st in each of next 3 ch-3 sps. At end of last row, fasten off.

LEFT SHOULDER
Row 1: With RS facing, sk next 7 ch-3 sps from Right Shoulder, join pigtail in next ch-3 sp, beg V-st in same sp, V-st in each of next 3 [3, 3, 5, 5, 5] ch-3 sps, turn.

Rows 2–5: Rep rows 2–5 of Right Shoulder.

BACK
Rnds 1–13 [1–13, 1–13, 1–17, 1–17, 1–17]: Rep rnds 1–13 [1–13, 1–13, 1–17, 1–17, 1–17] of Front.

RIGHT SHOULDER
Rows 1–4: Rep rows 1–4 of Right Shoulder of Front.

Row 5: Ch 1, sl st in next ch-3 sp, ch 4, drop lp from hook, insert hook in 2nd ch of corresponding ch-3 sp on front shoulder, pick up dropped lp and pull through, ch 1, dc in same sp on back shoulder, **V-st join** *(see Special Stitches)* in each of next 3 [3, 3, 5, 5, 5] ch-3 sps, leaving rem ch-3 sps unworked. Fasten off.

LEFT SHOULDER
Row 1: With RS facing, sk next 7 ch-3 sps from Right Shoulder, join pigtail in next ch-3 sp, beg V-st in same sp, V-st in each of next 3 [3, 3, 5, 5, 5] ch-3 sps, turn.

Rows 2–5: Ch 1, sl st in next ch-3 sp, beg V-st in same sp, V-st in each of next 3 ch-3 sps. At end of last row, fasten off.

FIRST FRONT SIDE SEAM
Row 1: With RS facing, join pigtail in center ch-3 sp at bottom left corner, beg V-st in same sp, V-st in each of next 11 [11, 11, 15, 15, 15] ch-3 sps, turn. *(12 [12, 12, 16, 16, 16] V-sts)*

Row 2: Ch 1, sl st in first ch-3 sp, beg V-st in same sp, V-st in each rem ch-3 sp across, turn.

Rep row 2, 0 [2, 4, 2, 3, 4] times. At end of last row, fasten off.

2ND FRONT SIDE SEAM

Row 1: With WS facing, join pigtail in center ch-3 sp at bottom right corner, beg V-st in same sp, V-st in each of next 11 [11, 11, 15, 15, 15] ch-3 sps, leaving rem ch-3 sps unworked, turn.

Row 2: Ch 1, sl st in first ch-3 sp, beg V-st in same sp, V-st in each rem ch-3 sp across, turn.

Rep row 2, 0 [2, 4, 2, 3, 4] times. At end of last row, fasten off.

FIRST BACK SIDE SEAM

Row 1: With RS facing, join pigtail in center ch-3 sp at bottom left corner, beg V-st in same sp, V-st in each of next 11 [11, 11, 15, 15, 15] ch-3 sps, turn. *(12 [12, 12, 16, 16, 16] V-sts)*

Rep row 2 of First Front Side Seam 0 [1, 2, 3, 4, 5] time(s).

Joining row: Sl st in first ch-3 sp, ch 4, drop lp from hook, insert hook in 2nd ch of corresponding ch-3 on front panel, pick up dropped lp and pull through, ch 1, dc in same ch-3 sp on back panel, (dc, **ch-3 join**—*see Special Stitches*, dc) in each of next 11 [11, 11, 15, 15, 15] ch-3 sps. Fasten off.

2ND SIDE SEAM

Row 1: With WS facing, join pigtail in center ch-3 sp at bottom right corner, beg V-st in same sp, V-st in each of next 11 [11, 11, 15, 15, 15] ch-3 sps, leaving rem ch-3 sps unworked, turn.

Rep row 2 of First Front Side Seam 0 [1, 2, 3, 4, 5] time(s).

Joining row: Rep joining row of First Back Side Seam.

NECK SHAPING

Rnd 1: Working in row ends of shoulders and ch-3 sps around neck opening, join turquoise in any row, ch 4, dc in same sp, (dc, ch 1, dc) in each row and ch-3 sp around, join in 3rd ch of beg ch-4. *(68 dc, 34 ch-3 sps)*

Rnds 2 & 3: Sl st in next ch-1 sp, ch 4, dc in same sp, (dc, ch 1, dc) in each ch-1 sp around, join in 3rd ch of beg ch-4. At end of last rnd, fasten off.

Rnd 4: With RS facing, join pigtail in any ch-1 sp, ch 1, (sc, ch 1, sc) in same sp and in each rem ch-1 sp around, join in beg sc.

Rnds 5 & 6: Sl st in next ch-1 sp, ch 1, (sc, ch 1, sc) in same sp and in each rem ch-1 sp around, join in beg sc. At end of last rnd, fasten off.

SLEEVE

Rnd 1: Working in row ends and ch-3 sps around armhole opening, join turquoise with sc in first row of side seam at underarm, ch 1, sc in same sp as beg ch-1, (sc, ch 1, sc) in each of next 3 [6, 9, 8, 10, 12] rows, (dc, ch 1, dc) in each of next 2 ch sps, (dc, ch 1, dc) in each of next 10 rows across shoulder, (dc, ch 1, dc) in each of next 2 ch sps, join in beg sc. *(8 [14, 20, 18, 22, 26] sc, 28 dc)*

Rnd 2: Sl st in next ch-1 sp, ch 1, sc in same sp as beg ch-1, sc in each of next 3 [6, 9, 8, 10, 12] ch-1 sps, (dc, ch 1, dc) in each rem ch-1 sp around, join in beg sc. *(4 [7, 10, 9, 11, 13] sc, 28 dc)*

Rnd 3: Sl st in next sc, ch 4, dc in same st as beg ch-4, [sk next sc, (dc, ch 1, dc) in next sc] 1 [2, 4, 3, 4, 5] time(s), (dc, ch 1, dc) in each ch-1 sp around, join in 3rd ch of beg ch-4. *(32 [34, 38, 36, 38, 40] dc)*

Rnds 4–29: Sl st in next ch-1 sp, ch 4, dc in same sp as beg ch-1, (dc, ch 1, dc) in each rem ch-1 sp around, join in 3rd ch of beg ch-4. At end of last rnd, fasten off.

Rnd 30: With RS facing, join pigtail with sc in any ch-1 sp, ch 1, sc in same sp as beg ch-1, (sc, ch 1, sc) in each rem ch-1 sp around, join in beg-sc.

Rnds 31 & 32: Sl st in next ch-1 sp, ch 1, (sc, ch 1, sc) in same sp as beg ch-1, (sc, ch 1, sc) in each rem ch-1 sp around, join in beg sc. At end of last rnd, fasten off.

BOTTOM BORDER

Rnd 1: With RS facing, join turquoise in first row of either side seam, ch 4, dc in same sp, (dc, ch 1, dc) in each row, (dc, ch 1, dc) in each ch-3 sp to 2nd Side Seam, (dc, ch 1, dc) in each row, (dc, ch 1, dc) in each rem ch-3 sp around, join in 3rd ch of beg ch-4.

Rnds 2–4: Sl st in next ch-1 sp, ch 4, dc in same sp, (dc, ch 1, dc) in each rem ch-1 sp around, join in 3rd ch of beg ch-4. At end of last rnd, fasten off.

Rnd 5: With RS facing, join pigtail with sc in any ch-1 sp, ch 1, sc in same sp as beg ch-1, (sc, ch 1, sc) in each rem ch-1 sp around, join in beg sc.

Rnds 6 & 7: Sl st in next ch-1 sp, ch 1, (sc, ch 1, sc) in same sp and in each rem ch-1 sp around, join in beg sc.

At end of last rnd, fasten off.

HAT

Rnds 1–9: Rep rnds 1–9 of Pullover.

Rnd 10: With RS facing, join tutu in ch-3 sp of next V-st, ch 6, V-st in same sp as beg ch-6, ch 3, *(dc, ch 3, V-st) in ch-3 sp of next V-st, ch 3, rep from * around, join in 3rd ch of beg ch-6. *(32 V-sts, 16 ch-3 sps)*

Rnd 11: Sl st in ch-3 sp of next V-st, beg V-st in same sp, V-st in each rem ch-3 sp around, join in 3rd ch of beg ch-6. Fasten off. *(48 V-sts)*

Rnd 12: With RS facing, join orchid in ch-3 sp of beg V-st, beg V-st in same sp, V-st in ch-3 sp of each rem V-st around, join in 3rd ch of beg ch-6.

Rnd 13: Sl st in next ch-3 sp, ch 1, 2 sc in same sp, 2 sc in each rem ch-3 sp around, join in beg sc. Fasten off. *(96 sc)*

Rnd 14: With RS facing, join pigtail with sc in any st, sc in each rem st around, join in beg sc.

Rnd 15: Ch 1, sc in each st around, join in beg sc.

Rnd 16: Ch 1, sc in same st as beg ch-1, **sc dec** *(see Stitch Guide)* in next 2 sts, *sc in next st, sc dec in next 2 sts, rep from * around, join in beg sc. *(64 sc)*

Rnds 17 & 18: Rep rnd 15.

Rnd 19: Ch 1, sc in same st as beg ch-1, *sc dec in next 2 sts, sc in next st, sc dec in next 2 sts, sc in each of next 4 sts, rep from * around, join in beg sc. *(51 sc)*

Rnd 20: Ch 1, sc in each st around, join in beg sc. Fasten off.

FINISHING

Immerse Pullover and Hat in cool water, squeeze out excess water, taking care not to wring or twist. Place on a flat, covered surface, gently stretching to open lace pattern. Leave until completely dry. ■

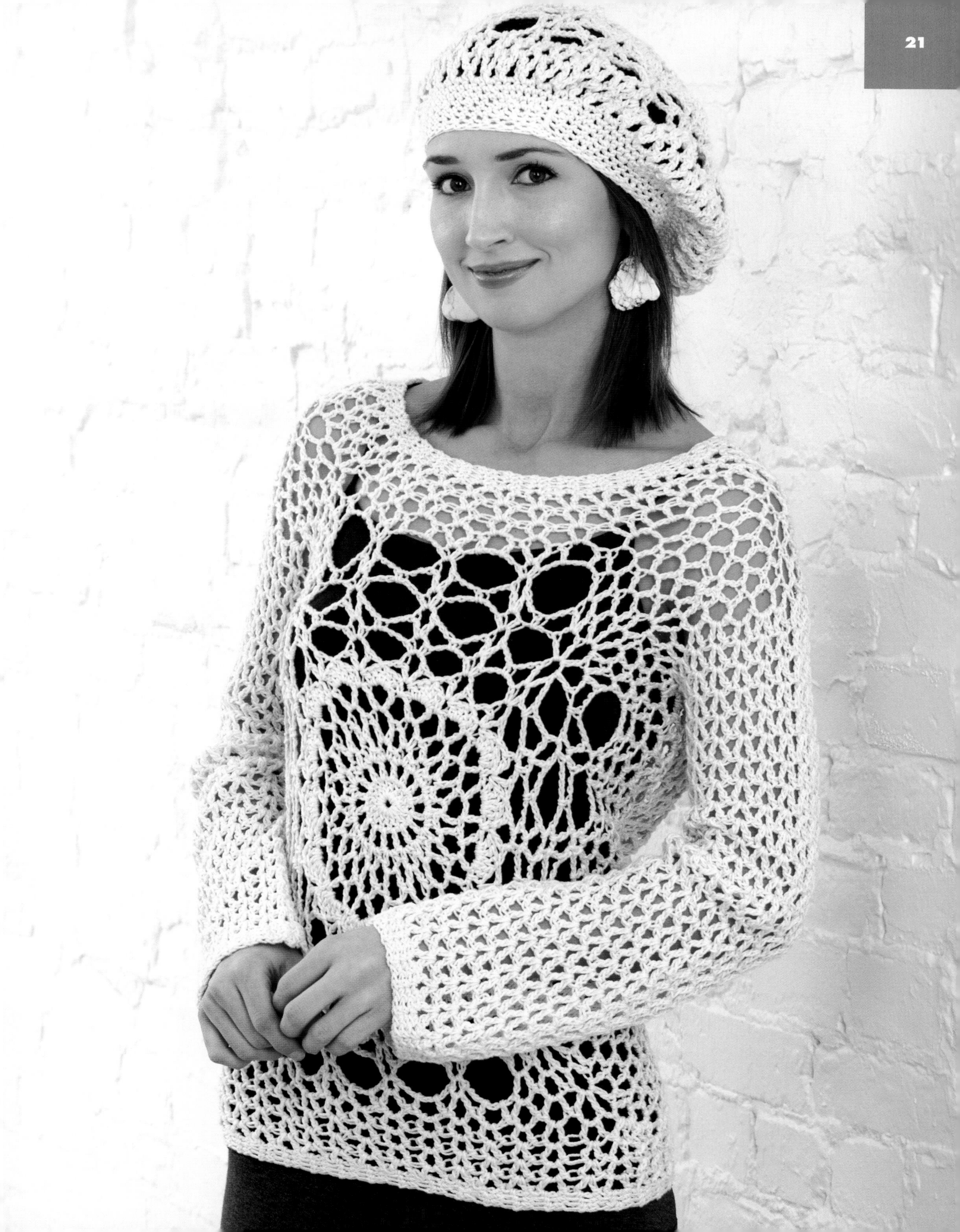

STITCH GUIDE

FOR MORE COMPLETE INFORMATION, VISIT **ANNIESCATALOG.COM/STITCHGUIDE**

STITCH ABBREVIATIONS

beg	begin/begins/beginning
bpdc	back post double crochet
bpsc	back post single crochet
bptr	back post treble crochet
CC	contrasting color
ch(s)	chain(s)
ch-	refers to chain or space previously made (i.e., ch-1 space)
ch sp(s)	chain space(s)
cl(s)	cluster(s)
cm	centimeter(s)
dc	double crochet (singular/plural)
dc dec	double crochet 2 or more stitches together, as indicated
dec	decrease/decreases/decreasing
dtr	double treble crochet
ext	extended
fpdc	front post double crochet
fpsc	front post single crochet
fptr	front post treble crochet
g	gram(s)
hdc	half double crochet
hdc dec	half double crochet 2 or more stitches together, as indicated
inc	increase/increases/increasing
lp(s)	loop(s)
MC	main color
mm	millimeter(s)
oz	ounce(s)
pc	popcorn(s)
rem	remain/remains/remaining
rep(s)	repeat(s)
rnd(s)	round(s)
RS	right side
sc	single crochet (singular/plural)
sc dec	single crochet 2 or more stitches together, as indicated
sk	skip/skipped/skipping
sl st(s)	slip stitch(es)
sp(s)	space(s)/spaced
st(s)	stitch(es)
tog	together
tr	treble crochet
trtr	triple treble
WS	wrong side
yd(s)	yard(s)
yo	yarn over

YARN CONVERSION

OUNCES TO GRAMS		GRAMS TO OUNCES	
1	28.4	25	⅞
2	56.7	40	1⅔
3	85.0	50	1¾
4	113.4	100	3½

UNITED STATES		UNITED KINGDOM
sl st (slip stitch)	=	sc (single crochet)
sc (single crochet)	=	dc (double crochet)
hdc (half double crochet)	=	htr (half treble crochet)
dc (double crochet)	=	tr (treble crochet)
tr (treble crochet)	=	dtr (double treble crochet)
dtr (double treble crochet)	=	ttr (triple treble crochet)
skip	=	miss

Single crochet decrease (sc dec): (Insert hook, yo, draw lp through) in each of the sts indicated, yo, draw through all lps on hook.

Example of 2-sc dec

Half double crochet decrease (hdc dec): (Yo, insert hook, yo, draw lp through) in each of the sts indicated, yo, draw through all lps on hook.

Example of 2-hdc dec

Reverse single crochet (reverse sc): Ch 1, sk first st, working from left to right, insert hook in next st from front to back, draw up lp on hook, yo and draw through both lps on hook.

Chain (ch): Yo, pull through lp on hook.

Single crochet (sc): Insert hook in st, yo, pull through st, yo, pull through both lps on hook.

Double crochet (dc): Yo, insert hook in st, yo, pull through st, [yo, pull through 2 lps] twice.

Double crochet decrease (dc dec): (Yo, insert hook, yo, draw lp through, yo, draw through 2 lps on hook) in each of the sts indicated, yo, draw through all lps on hook.

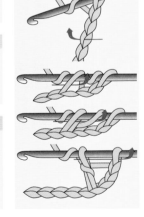

Example of 2-dc dec

Front loop (front lp) Back loop (back lp)

Front Loop   Back Loop

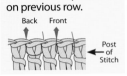

Front post stitch (fp): Back post stitch (bp): When working post st, insert hook from right to left around post of st on previous row.

Back   Front

← Post of Stitch

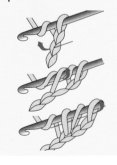

Half double crochet (hdc): Yo, insert hook in st, yo, pull through st, yo, pull through all 3 lps on hook.

Double treble crochet (dtr): Yo 3 times, insert hook in st, yo, pull through st, [yo, pull through 2 lps] 4 times.

Treble crochet decrease (tr dec): Holding back last lp of each st, tr in each of the sts indicated, yo, pull through all lps on hook.

Example of 2-tr dec

Slip stitch (sl st): Insert hook in st, pull through both lps on hook.

Chain color change (ch color change) Yo with new color, draw through last lp on hook.

Double crochet color change (dc color change) Drop first color, yo with new color, draw through last 2 lps of st.

Treble crochet (tr): Yo twice, insert hook in st, yo, pull through st, [yo, pull through 2 lps] 3 times.

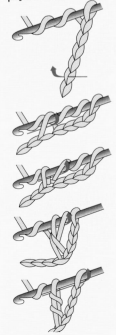

Metric Conversion Charts

METRIC CONVERSIONS

yards	x	.9144	=	metres (m)
yards	x	91.44	=	centimetres (cm)
inches	x	2.54	=	centimetres (cm)
inches	x	25.40	=	millimetres (mm)
inches	x	.0254	=	metres (m)

centimetres	x	.3937	=	inches
metres	x	1.0936	=	yards

INCHES INTO MILLIMETRES & CENTIMETRES (Rounded off slightly)

inches	mm	cm	inches	cm	inches	cm	inches	cm
1/8	3	0.3	5	12.5	21	53.5	38	96.5
1/4	6	0.6	5 1/2	14	22	56	39	99
3/8	10	1	6	15	23	58.5	40	101.5
1/2	13	1.3	7	18	24	61	41	104
5/8	15	1.5	8	20.5	25	63.5	42	106.5
3/4	20	2	9	23	26	66	43	109
7/8	22	2.2	10	25.5	27	68.5	44	112
1	25	2.5	11	28	28	71	45	114.5
1 1/4	32	3.2	12	30.5	29	73.5	46	117
1 1/2	38	3.8	13	33	30	76	47	119.5
1 3/4	45	4.5	14	35.5	31	79	48	122
2	50	5	15	38	32	81.5	49	124.5
2 1/2	65	6.5	16	40.5	33	84	50	127
3	75	7.5	17	43	34	86.5		
3 1/2	90	9	18	46	35	89		
4	100	10	19	48.5	36	91.5		
4 1/2	115	11.5	20	51	37	94		

KNITTING NEEDLES CONVERSION CHART

Canada/U.S.	0	1	2	3	4	5	6	7	8	9	10	10½	11	13	15
Metric (mm)	2	2¼	2¾	3¼	3½	3¾	4	4½	5	5½	6	6½	8	9	10

CROCHET HOOKS CONVERSION CHART

Canada/U.S.	1/B	2/C	3/D	4/E	5/F	6/G	8/H	9/I	10/J	10½/K	N
Metric (mm)	2.25	2.75	3.25	3.5	3.75	4.25	5	5.5	6	6.5	9.0

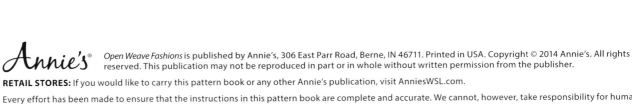